1
Gera
for the Garden

The material for this booklet has been provided by members of the Hardy Geranium Group of the Hardy Plant Society, to whom we are deeply grateful. Joy Jones would like to thank Peter Yeo for his support and advice. The booklet is designed to encourage those gardeners who have discovered the delights of this attractive genus and who want a little more information so that they can try more hardy geraniums in their gardens.

Line drawings by Peggy Dawe
Silhouettes by Joy Jones

Key to front cover.

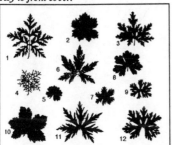

1. *Geranium rubescens*
2. *Geranium × riversleaianum* 'Russell Prichard'
3. *Geranium robustum*
4. *Geranium incanum*
5. *Geranium sessiliflorum* 'Nigricans'
6. *Geranium pulchrum*
7. *Geranium macrostylum*
8. *Geranium × cantabrigiense*
9. *Geranium orientalitibeticum*
10. *Geranium sinense*
11. *Geranium clarkei*
12. *Geranium pogonanthum*

ISBN 0 901687 06 5
First edition June 1992. Second edition April 1993
Further booklets on other genera will be published from time to time

Geranium pratense

Introduction

JOY JONES

TO many people, the name geranium still relates to the exotic, tender bedding plants, so popular in the Victorian era, which are now botanically, *Pelargonium*. Old habits die hard and so there is a lot of confusion when 'hardy geraniums' are mentioned. It is with these, the true *Geranium* or cranesbill (referring to the beak-like seed structure) that we are concerned in this booklet.

To confuse matters further, there are a few geraniums that are *not* entirely hardy in the British Isles. Nevertheless, the majority are able to withstand the coldest winters, easy to grow, practically disease-free, usually ignored by pests, tolerant of different soil conditions and able to thrive in sun or half shade (some deep shade).

Newcomers to gardening are well-advised to start with some of the 'easy' species, in the probability that they will then be encouraged to collect more varieties. My first introduction to gardening was on heavy blue clay (adjoining the local brick fields). Everything I planted rotted or was devoured by slugs or smothered by pernicious weeds — until someone gave me *Geranium × magnificum*, which did so well I was soon on the road to geranium addiction.

Although some species have been grown in our gardens for over four hundred years, recently their popularity has greatly increased. Today the choice is very much wider and discerning gardeners are realising that there is a geranium for every situation. They are ideal for informal cottage gardens, but equally at home in more formal plantings. Their leaves (which press well for close examination) vary in shape, size and texture; some are pleasantly aromatic, though herb robert, *G. robertianum*, is not so fragrant. It is, perhaps, the simplicity of the flowers that makes cranesbills so appealing and their ability to mingle delightfully with other plants.

You may ask if they have any disadvantages. One, possibly, is the profusion with which some species disperse their seedlings; this can be a problem, especially in small gardens. However, once you have learned to recognize the seedlings, unwanted ones are easily removed when small. If you have ground to spare, these can be grown on, just in case you have an exciting new hybrid. Another complaint is that some become untidy after the main flush of flowers, particularly *G. endressii* and *G. × oxonianum* and their forms. Shearing the foliage to the ground is the answer, resulting in a fresh crop of foliage and flowers, though watering in dry weather is advisable after this treatment.

1

Getting to know geraniums is an enjoyable pastime. Many can be seen by visiting specialist nurseries and botanic gardens. There is a National Collection of species at Cambridge Botanic Garden and cultivars can be seen at Cherry Hinton Hall nearby. Further National Collections are held at East Lambrook Manor, South Petherton, in Somerset and Catforth Gardens near Preston, run by Judith Bradshaw and Chris Moore.

Literature on geraniums is scarce. The late Margery Fish stimulated interest with her books, such as *Ground Cover Plants*, *Gardening in the Shade* and *Cottage Garden Flowers*. *Hardy Geraniums* by Dr Peter Yeo of Cambridge University was first published in 1985, after many years of research into the genus. This authoritative work has clarified the confusion surrounding previous naming of many species. It has also inspired gardeners to seek rarer varieties.

Further knowledge can be gained by joining specialist societies, such as The Hardy Plant Society, which runs a Hardy Geranium Group and there is the Geraniaceae Group of the British Pelargonium and Geranium Society.

Geranium renardii

Gregarious Geraniums

PAT COLLISON

WHENEVER I am asked 'What would look nice with ...?' one or more of the hardy geranium family immediately comes to mind. Versatile, colourful, hard-working and attractive in flower and foliage, you can find a geranium for every situation from rock-garden to mixed border, from woodland to meadow. This versatility, allied to a colour range of white, pale to deep pinks, mauves and blues, also makes geraniums perfect material for those of us who enjoy colour scheming and plant associations.

June is, traditionally, the month of roses. It is also the month when many of the most colourful geraniums are giving of their best and they make joyful companions. One of the easiest and most widely grown ('common' sounds so rude) is *G.* × *magnificum*, with sheaves of satin sheened violet blue flowers — just right for planting at the foot of a pink or yellow rose, together, perhaps, with *Lamium maculatum* 'Album' (or the silver-leaved *L. m.* 'White Nancy') and *Alchemilla mollis*. The daintier, blue-flowered *G.* 'Johnson's Blue' is equally lovely. Or, to increase the cool serenity of a white-flowered rose, plant beside it the geranium 'Mrs Kendall Clark', with beautifully veined light lavender-blue flowers and *Linaria purpurea* 'Canon Went' with slender spires of shell pink, rising above a foreground of grey cotton lavender and *G. sanguineum striatum* (syn. *G. lancastriense*). *G.* 'Mrs Kendall Clark' also looks lovely with the glaucous, ferny foliage and fluffy pale-lemon flowers of *Thalictrum flavum glaucum* (syn. *T. speciosissimum*) and, since their seasons sometimes overlap, it's worth adding a tall bearded iris in pale yellow or blue.

A delicate tracery of veining on the petals is a feature of many geraniums, but in some it is especially attractive. One such is *G. clarkei* 'Kashmir White', whose wide white flowers, poised on thread-like stems above finely cut leaves, have a shading of greyish pink, as though caught in a perpetual twilight of their own. This is a perfect companion for silver foliage, mauve-pink aquilegias, irises and clematis and old roses with cool, grey-washed pink and lavender blooms. The huge starry spheres of *Allium albopilosum* and the plump spires of *Penstemon* 'Sour Grapes' also make a nice group with *G. c.* 'Kashmir White'. *G. cinereum* 'Ballerina' with light lavender pink flowers, bewitchingly dark eyed and dark veined, could front the planting, interspersed with purple-leaved *Viola labradorica* or the black strap-like foliage of *Ophiopogon planiscapus nigrescens*.

Another geranium with beautifully veined twilight-white flowers is *G. renardii*. This has velvety-soft, grey-green leaves, rounded and lobed and it enjoys sun and good drainage, making it an ideal companion for *Nepeta mussinii* and old cottage pinks growing at the pathside.

Some kind of support is needed for most of the taller growing geraniums, at least while they are in bloom, but some produce long, slender, jointed stems that seem designed to meander gracefully into the lower branches of shrubs. One such is G. 'Brookside', whose rich blue, white-eyed flowers are produced through summer and well into autumn: lovely with pink, yellow, white or even orange roses, or the creamy-white and pale green variegated *Cornus alba* 'Elegantissima'. It also looks charming spreading amongst yellow flowered hemerocallis and green leaved yellow edged hostas. *Geranium wallichianum* 'Buxton's Variety' is another beautiful white-eyed blue which acts in a similar fashion, though on a smaller scale, and associates well with variegated mints, or with *Morina longifolia* and white flowered parahebes.

All blue geraniums have a tinge of violet, some more than others, and all the pinks lean towards the blue end of the spectrum (except *G. sanguineum striatum*). Nevertheless some can sizzle just as hotly as the brightest scarlet — *GG. psilostemon* and *cinereum* in particular are guaranteed to hold their own in the most flamboyant company. Because of their brilliance, care is needed when choosing neighbours. Silver, whites and blues are safe as well as attractive, but for anyone who can enjoy the barbaric splendour of massed clashing pinks, reds, oranges and magentas, they are totally irresistible. Less violent but still searingly bright, is the combination of magenta and yellow: for instance *G. psilostemon* with tall achilleas or a background of *Weigela* 'Looymansii Aurea' or *Cornus alba* 'Spaethii'. Given a plain evergreen background the magenta and yellow combination can be mellowed considerably by the addition of creamy plumed *Aruncus dioicus* (syn. *A. sylvester*) or the daintier *A. d.* 'Kneifii' and the green and white striped grass, *Phalaris arundinacea* var. *picta*.

The jazzy brilliance of *G. psilostemon* can be further soothed by planting it with *Lavatera* 'Barnsley', the tall blue-mauve *Nepeta* 'Six Hills Giant', *Salvia nemorosa* 'East Friesland' and *Artemisia* 'Lambrook Silver' or 'Powis Castle'. With a background of purple clematis and an edging of lavenders and santolinas and mauve and white violas, this would be a group with which even the most timid of us could relax.

Many of the geraniums make superb ground cover plants, one of the best being *G. macrorrhizum* in its varieties. Of these the rich magenta flowered *G. m.* 'Bevan's Variety' and the newer, but similar, 'Czakor' make showy carpets round yellow or white variegated shrubs, the silver *Pyrus salicifolia* 'Pendula' or interspersed with ferns, white flowered foxgloves and white edged *Hosta* 'Thomas Hogg' in shade under trees. The pink-flushed, white flowered *G. macrorrhizum* 'Album' looks especially attractive with mahogany leaved shrubs such as *Cotinus coggygria* 'Royal Purple' or *Berberis* × *ottawensis* 'Purpurea'.

4

Many geraniums grow equally well in sun or shade and are particularly valuable for their tolerance of dry shade. One such is *G. phaeum*, whose flowers include intriguingly dusky tones of reddish purplish black that beg to be combined with pale foxgloves, lamiums with silver splashed leaves, the white lacy umbels of sweet cicely (or even hedge parsley) and shrubs with yellow or white variegated foliage.

Even when not in flower geraniums make worthy contributions to the garden scene with their maple-like leaves, broadly or finely cut, contrasting nicely with the narrow foliage of ornamental grasses, irises and hermerocallis, the wide leaves of hostas and bergenias, or the silver filigree of artemisias and santolinas. Who, in fairness, could ask for more?

Geranium macrorrhizum

5

Hardy Geraniums for Foliage Effect

TREVOR BATH

HARDY geraniums are usually spoken of in terms of their flowers, which come in a good range of colours and are often produced for weeks on end.

This aspect of the plants has rather diverted attention from the leaves, which provide many variations on a theme. The basic leaf shape is a five-pointed one. Sometimes the sections have shallow notches and indentations, but more often they are divided and sub-divided into all sorts of pleasing and variant patterns. The size, and sometimes the shape, varies between the main, basal leaves and any leaves borne on the flowering stems. With some of the smaller growing varieties, the leaves give a general impression of being more circular than pointed, but within that shape the divisions tend to be more intricate and lacy.

There are only a few hardy geranium leaves with variegation, but there are infinite gradations of green, sometimes two shades of green on the same leaf. In some varieties the young leaves in spring, or the old leaves in autumn, are distinguished by brilliant colours of red, yellow or cream. Others are noteworthy for attractive spots or blotches, or distinctive veining.

There is a suitable hardy geranium for any position in the garden. Here is a representative selection of just a few foliage varieties with particularly interesting details, although every variety has its own interest. They all repay close study and I do not believe there is a dull leaf among them.

SMALL-LEAVED VARIETIES

G. argenteum Outstanding for its small silvery leaves, a characteristic transmitted to its hybrid with *G. cinereum*, *G. × lindavicum*, of which the varieties *G. × l.* 'Apple Blossom' and *G. × l.* 'Lissadell' are particularly attractive. All of these are on such a miniature scale that they really need to be grown in containers, sinks or on scree beds so that they can be fully appreciated.

G. × cantabrigiense This hybrid between *G. macrorrhizum* and *G. dalmaticum* has shiny leaves like a larger version of the latter, with an aromatic quality derived from the former. It makes a compact mat. The other hybrid from the same cross, *G. × cantabrigiense* 'Biokovo', which occurred naturally in the former Yugoslavia, has slightly larger leaves, but is not so close-growing.

G. dalmaticum Small, neat shiny leaves which colour well in the autumn, especially in the sunny, well-drained site it prefers.

G. orientalitibeticum G. stapfianum roseum misapplied. Worth growing if only for the sake of its new name; a little practice enables you to bring it forth trippingly on the tongue. A low growing plant with nicely divided leaves in green (two shades) and yellow, which dies down at the end of the summer; it can increase quite rapidly by the multiplication of its strange, bead-like roots. If allowed some space, an established colony can look delightful as an underplanting for *Sisyrinchium striatum* or sedums.

G. renardii I have no hesitation in naming this as my number one favourite. The unique leaves are a soft sage green, velvety to the touch, with a distinctive scalloped shape. It forms a neat, low mound, gradually increasing without ever becoming invasive. I would even forego the flowers, attractive as they are, for the sheer delight of the leaves.

G. sanguineum Both the species and the named varieties have masses of small, intricately cut leaves, and given a situation in a wall or paving will mound up nicely and form a superb foil to the flowers. In the autumn the leaves come into their own, when brilliant colours emphasise and dramatise the filigree shapes, so that they look like sprays of burning snow crystals.

G. sessiliflorum 'Nigricans' Not everyone's cup of tea (or coffee might be more appropriate). A low growing dense clump of small dun-coloured leaves, occasionally highlighted by an intriguing orange one. A difficult plant to place since its dull colour needs displaying against a lighter coloured background — gravel or paving — to make it more effective. A challenge to ingenuity with plant associations; low growing plants with gold leaves such as *Lysimachia nummularia* 'Aurea', *Veronica prostrata* 'Trehane', variagated arabis or the small, variegated form of London pride would all give it a lift. Or make a virtue of its greyish brown colour by adding even darker plants; *Ophiopogon planiscapus nigrescens, Ajuga reptans* 'Atropurpurea', *Trifolium repens* 'Purpurascens' or *Viola labradorica*. The geranium foliage overwinters well. I have seen even more desirable forms with deep red leaves.

MEDIUM-LEAVED VARIETIES

G. 'Ann Folkard' This hybrid from *G. procurrens* and *G. psilostemon* has the trailing habit of the former, but without the ability to root as it goes along. The young leaves have a distinctive golden flush, well displayed when grown through a shrub or mounded up in paving.

G. dahuricum Finely cut leaves with long narrow divisions. The new leaves in spring are a delicate pink and cream and the mature leaves are often red edged.

G. incanum Very finely dissected, greyish leaves on trailing stems give an elegant effect. Unfortunately it is not entirely hardy (it comes from South Africa) but can be kept going by overwintering cuttings.

G. malviflorum G.atlanticum misapplied. Outstanding for its unusual life style: the finely cut leaves appear in September and provide a useful patch of hardy green throughout the winter. If grown in a sunny well-drained spot, they will be joined by spectacular flowers in May, then the whole plant dies down for a summer rest. If grown in a shady situation where it fails to flower, I think it is still well worth growing for its overwintering foliage alone.

G. nodosum My number two favourite. Very attractive bright green shiny leaves, five-lobed at the base, three-lobed on the flowering stems. At first glance it could be mistaken for an astrantia. Good in shade.

G. robustum Another plant of which I am very fond, and which is now being more widely distributed. The narrowly divided grey-green leaves, rather sparsely held on angular stems, look rather more like one of the daintier scented pelargoniums than a geranium. It is alleged to be not entirely hardy, but it has survived unprotected in my garden in Surrey for many years and occasionally even produces a seedling.

G. versicolor A low growing plant, the fresh green leaves are marked on each lobe with a brown spot and usually stay green through the winter. Good for the wild garden, it hybridizes freely with *G.endressii*, with some of the resulting by-blows being worthier than others.

G. wallichianum The type plant is rarely seen, having been displaced by the more fashionable *G.* 'Buxton's Variety', but it is by no means to be despised, with its trailing stems of dark green, mottled leaves which take on brilliant red tones in the autumn.

LARGE-LEAVED VARIETIES

G. macrorrhizum The handsome, broadly lobed leaves are a good background for the flowers and are semi-evergreen, with reddish tinges in autumn and winter. Oil of geranium was once extracted from the aromatic leaves. Of course, sense of smell being such a personal thing, some visitors to the garden recoil in horror when a leaf is waved under their noses. The variegated form is very special with good creamy-yellow markings, but it is a plant which refuses to grow well for me. I was very envious of an excellent clump I saw in a garden in Lincoln where it was growing in a shady well-watered border, beautifully associated with variegated ajuga and a blue hosta.

G. maderense The species with the largest and most spectacular leaf. The big, rather ferny leaves cover a wide area, the leaf stalks eventually leaning their elbows on the ground to support the luxuriant top growth. Originating from Madeira, it needs shelter, preferably under glass in a large greenhouse or a very large container, to give of its best.

G. × oxonianum 'Claridge Druce' Quickly makes a large clump of dramatic dark-green, spotted leaves. If only it stopped there! Apart from hybridizing promiscuously and seeding about prolifically, it makes such a strong plant, with very tenacious roots, that a pickaxe is needed to dislodge it. But it is an excellent subject for the wild garden or woodland where it can be left alone to produce a striking show of substantial leaves for most of the year.

G. phaeum 'Variegatum' *G. punctatum* 'Variegatum' misapplied. Splendid edgings and markings of cream and red on dark green background, very subtle and attractive. Some clones seem to have more constant variegation than others, which revert to plain green at the height of the season, but a severe haircut will usually produce a good second crop of variegated leaves.

G. platyanthum (syn. *G. eriostemon*) Strongly textured dark green leaves, the shape being reminiscent of hollyhock leaves. Good autumn colour.

G. pratense Large, well-cut leaves which sometimes suffer from mildew in a dry season, around the time when the flowers are fading: this is another plant which benefits from being cut right to the ground at that time, to stimulate fresh new growth. If interplanted with colchicums, the spring leaves will help to disguise the decaying bulb leaves in their prolonged death throes, then, after their midsummer trim, the second batch of geranium leaves will make a tactful accompaniment to the bare-stemmed colchicum flowers.

G. psilostemon The big heraldic leaves associate well with shrubs and are notable for splendid autumn colour. In additon, the emerging leaf buds and stipules in spring are a brilliant red.

Geraniums as Ground Cover

JUDITH BRADSHAW

WITH their attractive foliage and flowers, easy cultivation and propagation and their ability to spread quickly and smother weeds, geraniums must be among the best of ground cover plants. I grow them in many parts of the garden and by careful selection can have both flowers and easy maintenance from spring to late autumn.

In shady areas *G. phaeum* and its varieties form evergreen clumps and the dainty muted flowers look lovely from April to June; *G. monacense* and *G. reflexum,* its close relatives, are just as effective. The flowers of *G. macrorrhizum* follow in May, where even in my dry shadiest areas they bloom well. Pale pink *G. m.* 'Ingwersen's Variety' and magenta *G. m.* 'Czakor' give me the best cover; they will grow equally well in sun and their aromatic foliage colours well in the autumn.

By the end of May *G. endressii* and its cultivar, 'Wargrave Pink', start flowering and continue until the frosts. *G. versicolor* gives paler flowers but similar cover, or *G. × oxonianum* in varying shades of pink, gives stronger, larger clumps. *G. × o.* 'Claridge Druce' is the most vigorous but 'A. T. Johnson' and 'Rose Clair' also grow well for me in shade. A little later the shiny leaves and wiry-stemmed flowers of *G. nodosum* spread in shady places, although I found this was slow to establish at first. *G. procurrens* flowers from July to November but is only safe for dry shady areas under tall shrubs; I grow it under a large rhus and conifers where it scrambles happily, masking the foliage of spring bulbs with its purple, black-centred flowers.

In sunnier borders my tall clumps of *G. sylvaticum* flower in May and June. Their soft colours blend well with early summer flowers, whilst under an unfurling birch, *G. s.* 'Mayflower' gives a lovely display of violet blue. Later the leaves give attractive background cover. At the front of this border the pale, veined flowers of *G. renardii* stand above sage-green, velvety leaves which give interesting textured mounds of foliage all season, whilst further back *G. clarkei* 'Kashmir White' grows in partial shade, its large white, purple-veined petals appearing almost luminous and its rhizomes creeping steadily to make a solid patch. *G. clarkei* 'Kashmir Purple' smothers a square yard (metre) of ground in full sun where the lovely glowing flowers associate well with white and greys.

During May and June a rich blue carpeter flowers in a sunny border: *G. himalayense* and its cultivar 'Gravetye' make dense masses of low foliage and large flowers. One of my favourites is the purplish-pink double form,

G. h. 'Plenum' but it takes much longer to make a thick carpet. The tall clump forming *G.pratense* also flowers in June in shades of blue, pink and white and is useful planted where the large umbrellas of leaves can grow up in front of the spent foliage of daffodils. The most vigorous is *G. pratense albiflorum*, a magnificent sight with its large white flowers rising to 3ft (90cm). I use the *G. himalayense* × *G. pratense* hybrid, 'Johnson's Blue' with its large blue flowers as a carpeter among shrubs or at the edge of borders. A very neat edger is the *G. macrorrhizum* × *G. dalmaticum* hybrid, *G.* × *cantabrigiense*; only 8in (20cm) high, with its aromatic evergreen foliage, it makes a low weed-proof barrrier with masses of pink flowers in early summer. It flowers less well in shade and although I grow the paler form, *G.* × *c.* 'Biokovo', I don't find it as successful as ground cover, being slower to establish and less compact.

In June also, the showiest of the blue geraniums are in bloom. *G. platypetalum* and its hybrid with *G. ibericum*, *G.* × *magnificum* have a three week burst of intense flowering and although their season is short compared to many geraniums they give a brilliant display in the June garden and impenetrable cover for the rest of the season, with autumn colour to follow. Their purplish-blue colour associates well with *G. psilostemon*, a lovely plant for a sunny border, forming a mound of large attractive leaves and long blooming, black-eyed, magenta flowers. Its cultivar, *G.p.* 'Bressingham Flair', has slightly softer colouring but not the same ground covering qualities. In the same bed the exotic *G.palmatum*, with its massive evergreen rosette of leaves smothers a wide area, its pink flowers reaching up to 3ft (90cm). I didn't expect it to provide me with good cover as it is considered slightly tender, but temperatures of -10° C last winter left it unscathed.

In slight shade a mound of the attractive *G. wlassovianum* covers the ground and nearby, also in shade, creeps *G. lambertii*. One of the longest flowerers, the lovely hybrid *G.* × *riversleaianum* 'Russell Prichard' needs full sun and sharp drainage. It covers the ground with trails of greyish foliage and bright pink flowers which last from June till the frosts and mingle with the nearby bushy mass of *G. sanguineum* 'Album'.

The sanguineums make ideal cover for the front of borders, raised beds or rockeries. Besides the vivid magenta of the species the softer shades of *G. s.* 'Glenluce', 'Shepherd's Warning' and *G. s. striatum* give colour after the first flush of rockery flowers are finished. The *G. cinereum* cultivars like similar positions. *G. c.* 'Ballerina' and 'Laurence Flatman' have lovely veined petals whilst *G. cinereum subcaulescens* and its cultivar 'Splendens' give brighter patches of colour. Even lower is *G. dalmaticum*, a pale pink carpeter. Two other carpeters which enjoy scree conditions but are too invasive among small plants (as I found to my cost) are *G. orientalitibeticum* and its relative, *G. pylzowianum*. I now use these at the front of sun-baked borders among taller plants where they smother weeds without being troublesome.

Finally, one of the latest to flower, but one of my favourites, is *G. wallichianum* 'Buxton's Variety', with its china blue, white-centred, flowers, which blooms from late July to the frosts. At the front of my borders in sun and shade its flowers and marbled foliage take me well into autumn.

Cultivation
JOY JONES

MOST geraniums will grow in any reasonable soil in sun or half-shade. Any particular requirements are dealt with in the general list.

PESTS

Aphids: not often troublesome out of doors, but whitefly can be a nuisance in the greenhouse. I dislike using insecticides but in this case it seems to be the only way.

Slugs and Snails: may damage foliage, but they are not usually a serious problem.

Vine Weevils: lay their eggs on the soil and the resulting grubs are short, fat and white. They live on the roots, causing foliage to become sickly and wilt. Plants in pots are most at risk, especially in damp, peat-based compost. Suspect plants should be removed and if grubs are found, every scrap of soil washed off the roots with an appropriate insecticide. Replant in fresh soil or compost and clean pots. In the garden, water infested soil with insecticide, picking out and destroying as many grubs as you can find. They are very persistent and may need several doses at intervals.

DISEASES

These are few.

Rust: occasionally affects foliage, which should be removed and destroyed. If badly infected, spray with fungicide or special rust control or destroy the plant and start again.

Powdery Mildew: occurs mostly in very dry weather. Some forms of *G. pratense* are susceptible. Prevention is better than cure and regular division helps. Cut mildewed foliage to the ground, dust with Flowers of Sulphur and keep well-watered.

Virus: attacks a few species causing distortion of petals. Destroy infected plants and watch seedlings, as the virus can be carried to future generations.

Propagation
REX HARPER

DIVISION OF CLUMPS

With established stocks of geraniums this is by far the easiest way to increase one's plants. It is quite practical to lift a whole clump of a species such as *G. endressii* in the early spring, pull it apart and re-plant sufficient material to make a colourful show during the coming summer. The root divisions can then either be planted out into their flowering positions or potted on to provide stock for exchanges or plant sales.

Most of the vigorous, clump forming species of geraniums can be divided in the above manner but remember to water for a while after re-planting, if the weather is dry. Personally I feel that it is not a good idea to divide clumps too early in their lives and I would recommend doing this every third year, rather than on a yearly basis; this applies in particular to the *G. pratense* varieties which always look their best in large, established clumps.

REMOVAL OF SIDE SHOOTS

Spreading species such as *GG. macrorrhizum, clarkei* and *dalmaticum* produce many side shoots which can be removed, often with roots attached. These will quickly make new plants and may well flower during the same season if they are planted out in the spring. In the case of the white form of *G. dalmaticum*, which is slow to grow from side shoots and dislikes our wet winters, side shoots are best taken in the autumn and grown on in small pots in a cold frame or greenhouse and planted out in their flowering positions in the spring.

DIVISION OF TUBERS

GG. pylzowianum, orientalitibeticum, malviflorum and other geraniums which produce tubers can be propagated simply by digging carefully around the main clump and removing small tubers, all of which will grow. Because of the speed with which some of the smaller mountain tuberous-rooted species increase they can present a problem in a rock garden but can be controlled if planted in pots which are sunk into the soil. Many seem to flower better if grown this way; maybe they prefer to be somewhat cramped, as they would be in a mountain crevice.

CUTTINGS

Varieties of geranium which produce long, trailing, but non-rooting stems such as *G.* 'Ann Folkard' and *G. wallichianum* can be grown from stem cuttings taken early in the growing season. The cuttings should comprise a node with about half an inch of stem on either side. Remove all but one leaf from the cutting and plant in shallow pots in a mixture of John Innes No. 2 and sharp sand, making sure that the soil is moistened and well firmed down before the cuttings are inserted. The cuttings are then planted flat, covering the stem with soil and allowing just the top of the node to protrude above the soil. Place the pots of cuttings in a cold frame or greenhouse and remember not to let them dry out. Pot on the young plants after they have made reasonable growth.

Some of the clump forming mountain geraniums, such as *G. cinereum* and its many varieties, will eventually make quite woody stems and these provide cuttings which can be obtained with the help of a sharp blade, by cutting small sections, each with two or three small leaves at the top, from the parent plant. These cuttings can be taken throughout the growing season and are best planted in pots of well-firmed John Innes No. 2 allowing the cutting to make its own hole in the compost and firming it in with the fingers, just below the leaves. Grow on in a cold frame or greenhouse.

SEED

Growing geraniums from seed can be a fascinating way of propagating your stock, that is if you are prepared to wait a while for the plants to bloom. Although some species like the *G. endressii* and *G. pratense* varieties will give plenty of flowers in the first year from seed, others take at least twelve months to get established before they even think of producing blooms.

Most species seem to germinate well if the seed is sown in a gritty soil compost. John Innes No. 2 with added grit makes a good medium. Water the compost well before sowing the seed thinly on the surface, cover with a dusting of sifted soil and place a sheet of glass over the tray or pot (remembering to leave an air space between the glass and the pot). Keep paper over the glass until the seeds start to germinate, at which time remove both paper and glass and place the trays or pots in a light place in the greenhouse or frame, to encourage growth.

Seedlings can be potted when the second pair of leaves are well developed and can then be grown on in pots until established. Remember to label each pot carefully as it is all too easy to get varieties mixed up.

Before planting out the seedlings in the garden read up on the varieties that you have grown and find out how each particular geranium would prefer to grow in the wild, then try to copy the type of habitat in your garden. A lot of disappointment can be overcome by taking a little care in positioning plants and not just putting them in odd corners in the hope

14

that they will grow.

Sometimes germination may be prolonged and often one finds seedlings coming up in pots which contain old compost which has been re-used, which can be most confusing. Therefore give your seeds plenty of time to get going before you give up and empty out the pots. Sometimes placing the pots on a shelf in the greenhouse fairly near the glass seems to help, but don't forget to water them.

Geranium cinereum 'Ballerina'

15

List of Geraniums in Cultivation

JOY JONES

THE following list includes only those geraniums known to be in cultivation, but by no means all. A few will be difficult to track down, though fortunately there are now several excellent nurseries specializing in hardy geraniums. It is also worth while searching through seed lists.

The name of the species is followed by: other names under which it may be found; its parentage if a hybrid; places of origin; approximate height (which will obviously vary according to soil and situation) and flowering time (again variable). Flower size refers to the approximate diameter.

SYMBOLS

Prop = propagation, C = cuttings, RC = root cuttings, D = division, S = seed and T = tubers.
* = easy geraniums for beginners

PERENNIALS

G. albanum SE Caucasus and adjacent parts of Iran. 12-18in (30-45cm). June onwards.
Forms substantial clumps of evergreen kidney-shaped, divided leaves from compact rootstock. Flowers ¾-1in (approx. 2cm) on long thin, trailing stems, rather chilly pink with magenta veins and slightly notched petals. Narrowly misses being a good garden plant due to its untidy habit, but useful for its long flowering period in woodland, wild garden or shrub border, where it will weave through neighbouring branches.
Prop: D or S

G. albiflorum N. & C. Asia, NE European Russia. 12in (30cm). May onwards.
A low growing, modest but charming plant with deeply divided leaves; stems, leaf margins and sepals purplish brown. Flowers, small, funnel-shaped, white or palest lilac, violet veined, notched petals, produced spasmodically over a long period. Prefers light shade.
Prop: D or S

G. anemonifolium see *G. palmatum*

G. 'Ann Folkard' (*G. procurrens* × *G. psilostemon*) A sterile hybrid raised by Revd Oliver Folkard in Lincolnshire (1973). An outstanding, much sought-after plant, producing a mass of golden-tinted foliage in spring from a comparatively small crown, later turning green. Very long, thin

non-rooting stems, cover a wide area, scrambling through other plants. Flowers 1½-1¾in (approx. 4cm) sumptuous rich purple, shot with pink, black centre and veins. Seems to change colour according to the light. Non-stop flowering from July to autumn.
Prop: D (in spring — care needed) or RC

G. 'Apple Blossom' see *G.* × *lindavicum*

G. argenteum French Alps, Italy, the former Yugoslavia. 4-6in (10-15cm). July-August.
A choice species for the rock garden, scree, trough or alpine house. Neat rosettes of small rounded, divided leaves covered with silvery silky hairs. Flowers 1in (2.5cm), white or pale pink with darker veins and slightly notched petals. Gritty soil in full sun, needing protection from winter wet.
Prop: D or C (with care), RC or S (may not come true)

G. argenteum × **G. cinereum** see *G.* × *lindavicum*

G. aristatum Mountains of S.Albania, S. of the former Yugoslavia, NW Greece. 18in (45cm). June-August
A distinctive hairy plant, forming hummocks of greyish-green leaves. Flowers 1in (2.5cm) nodding, petals strongly reflexed, white or pale lilac, attractively veined with violet. Reliable and worthy of a place in the border. Sun or part shade.
Prop: D or S (seed may be difficult to germinate: Dr Yeo suggests chipping seeds before sowing)

G. asphodeloides * S. Europe. 12-18in (30-45cm). June onwards.
Somewhat variable, makes substantial mounds of fresh-looking, evergreen rounded leaves for wild garden, banks, walls. Sun or shade.

G. asphodeloides subsp. *asphodeloides*
Starry flowers 1in (2.5cm) pale to deep mauvish pink, strongly veined with reddish purple. Rather gappy petals. There is also a white form.

G. asphodeloides subsp. *crenophilum*
Flowers rose pink with broad petals.

G. asphodeloides subsp. *sintenisii*
A very free-flowering plant with flowers a pale pink or purple.

G. 'Brookside' (probably *G. pratense* × *G. clarkei*) 24in (60cm). June-August.
A recently introduced hybrid, making clumps of finely cut foliage on reddish stems. Flowers large bowl-shaped of excellent deep blue, white at the centre. A lovely plant for sun or part shade.
Prop: D

G. canariense Canary Islands. 24in (60cm). Spring onwards.
Basal rosette of handsome, deeply divided large aromatic leaves, growing

17

from a stem a few inches above the soil. Leaf stalks flushed brownish purple. Numerous flowers 1½in (4cm) deep pink, rather widely spaced petals, pale on the underside, nearly white or dark at the base. Not fully hardy and short-lived (up to three years). Greenhouse or warm sheltered corner in well-drained soil in milder areas.
Prop: S

G. × *cantabrigiense (G. dalmaticum* × *G. macrorrhizum)* 12in (30cm). June-July.
Cheerful, compact mats of glossy, aromatic, evergreen foliage, spreading steadily, but not rampantly. Flowers 1in (2.5cm) bright pink, abundantly produced. Leaves and flowers midway between parents. *G.* × *c.* 'Biokovo' is less compact and not so vigorous with white, slightly pink-tinged flowers. Both good ground cover, front of the border, large rock garden in sun or part shade.
Prop: D (sterile)

G. cataractarum S. Spain, Morocco. 8-12in (30cm). June onwards.
A pretty plant with aromatic, deeply divided ferny leaves: evergreen. Flowers ¾in (2cm), funnel-shaped, bright pink with orange-red anthers. Rock garden or trough in half shade. Moderately hardy, though not very long-lived.
Prop: S

G. cinereum Central Pyrenees. 6in (15cm). June onwards.
Neat rosettes of small, rounded, divided leaves of greyish green. Flowers 1½in (4cm) on lax stems, white or pink, finely pencilled with darker veins. There is a pure white form. Rock garden, scree or trough. Gritty soil in sun.
Prop: D or S (seedlings may vary if other forms grown)

G. c. 'Ballerina' * Flowers 1¼in (3cm) purplish pink, petals notched, covered with a strong network of dark veins and dark blotch at the base. Most attractive and reliable. Raised by Blooms of Bressingham.
Prop: D or C

G. c. 'Lawrence Flatman' * Another winner from Blooms, similar to *G. c.* 'Ballerina' but with dark blotches near the top of the petals.

G. cinereum var. *subcaulescens* Balkan Peninsula,
C. & NE Turkey. 9in (22cm). May onwards.
Low-growing mounds of small, rounded, dark green leaves. Flowers 1in (2.5cm) fierce magenta, very dark centre and dark veins, black anthers. Rock garden, but keep well away from red-flowered plants! *G. c. s.* 'Giuseppii' has rather more silvery leaves, near magenta flowers with less pronounced central area. *G. c. s* . 'Splendens' flowers less strident in colour,

18

dark centre, nicely veined.
Prop: D or C

G. 'Claridge Druce' see *G.* × *oxonianum*

G. *clarkei* Kashmir. 18in (45cm). June onwards.

Two cultivars generally grown, both spreading by underground rhizomes producing finely cut, feathery leaves. Sun or part-shade.

G. c. 'Kashmir Purple' ⋆ (syn. *G. pratense* 'Kashmir Purple') *G. bergianum* misapplied. Spreads rapidly and can be invasive. Good groundcover for large areas. Flowers 1½in (approx. 4cm), facing upwards, deep violet purple, red veins.
Prop: D or S

G. c. 'Kashmir White' ⋆ *G. rectum album* misapplied. A beautiful plant, less vigorous than its purple counterpart. Flowers 1½-1¾in (approx. 4cm), white with delicate lilac-pink veins, giving a mauvish-grey flush to the petals.
Prop: D or S (some seedlings may revert to purple)

G. *collinum* ⋆   SE Europe, C. & E. Turkey, W. & C. Asia.
18-24in (45-60cm).   All summer.
Bushy clumps of deeply divided and finely cut grey-green leaves, sometimes primrose yellow tinged with pink in spring. Flowers 1-1½in (approx. 3cm), saucer-shaped, usually mid-pink, but can be lighter or darker. Useful in the border for its long flowering period and resistance to drought conditions.
Prop: D or S

G. *dahuricum* NE Asia, W. China. 18in (45cm). June-August.
A sprawler with thin lax stems, small finely cut leaves with narrow, rather widely spaced lobes. New leaves emerging in spring are delicate pink and cream. Flowers 1¼in (3cm), saucer-shaped pale pink with dark red veins. Large rock garden or wild garden in full sun.
Prop: D or S

G. *dalmaticum* SW of the former Yugoslavia, Albania. 4-6in
(10-15cm). June-July.
Dwarf, slowly spreading, neat hummocks of small, evergreen, aromatic shiny leaves. Flowers ¾-1in (approx. 2cm), lovely shell pink, held well above the foliage. Needs frequent division. Rock garden, trough or paving in sun. Good autumn tints.
Prop: D or RC

G. *dalmaticum* 'Album' A desirable white form, though less vigorous.

G. *donianum* Himalayas, SW China, Tibet. 6-18in (15-45cm).   Kid-

ney-shaped, deeply divided, marbled leaves from thick rootstock. Flowers funnel-shaped, upwardly inclined, reddish purple. Not very long-lived but easily raised from seed. Rather lost in the flower border, best in rock garden.
Prop: S

G. endressii * S. Europe, W. Asia. 18in (45cm). June-September.
Leafy clumps of almost evergreen, light green, divided and attractively pointed leaves, providing dense colonizing ground cover. Flowers 1-1½in (approx. 3cm), funnel-shaped, bright chalky pink with notched petals, over a very long period. Cut to the ground towards end of July, when becoming untidy, to produce fresh growth and flowers. Front of the border, light woodland, under shrubs, especially old roses.
Prop: D or S (may not come true)

G. e.'Wargrave Pink' (syn. *G. e.* 'Wargrave Variety') A taller form having warm salmon-pink flowers. Vigorous.

G. endressii × *G. versicolor* see *G.* × *oxonianum*

G. erianthum E. Siberia, Japan, Alaska, Canada (N.British Columbia). 18-24in (45-60cm). May-June and later.
Resembles *G. platyanthum* (syn. *G. eriostemon*) but leaves more deeply divided; divisions overlapping with numerous sharply pointed lobes and teeth. Good autumn colour. Flowers 1½in (4cm), flattish, varying from pale to rich violet blue and darkly veined. A plant of great charm for border, light woodland and beneath shrubs in sun or part shade.
Prop: D or S

G. eriostemon see *G. platyanthum*

G. farreri W. China. 4-6in (10-15cm). May-June.
Introduced by Farrer in 1917. A gem for the rock garden, scree, trough or alpine house; small, rounded, divided leaves, reddish margins and stems. Flowers 1-1½in (approx. 3cm) exquisite soft pink and conspicuous, bluish-black anthers. Well drained, light sandy/gritty soil in full sun.
Prop: D (by careful division of crowns with tap-root attached) or S

G. fremontii Western N. America. 12-18in (30-45cm). June-September.
A distinctive, sticky hairy geranium with numerous deeply divided leaves, coarsely lobed and toothed. Flowering stems much branched and leafy. Flowers 1½in (4cm), flat, upward facing, pale to deep pink, petals usually notched. Needs frequent re-planting as roots tend to become exposed. Rather too large and untidy for the average rock garden, though useful for its long flowering period in a sunny border. Self-sown seedlings occur occasionally.

Prop: D or S

G. glaberrimum Mountains of SW Turkey. 8in (20cm). June and later.
Little known species that would be suitable for the alpine house. Small kidney-shaped leaves. Flowers ¾in (2cm) bright pink with red anthers.
Prop: S

G. gracile NE Turkey, Caucasus. 18-24in (45-60cm). All summer.
Resembles *G. nodosum* but taller and hairier. Leaves light green, wrinkled with diamond-shaped divisions. Flowers funnel-shaped delicate pink, enhanced by fascinating short 'eyelash' veins. A graceful plant indeed for woodland or shady corners.
Prop: D or S

G. grevilleanum see *G.lambertii*

G. gymnocaulon NE Turkey, SW Caucasus. 12-18in (30-45cm). July-August
Allied to *G. ibericum* but less vigorous and later flowering. Flowers 1½in (4cm), rich violet blue with darker veins and notched petals. Tends to be rather short-lived. Large rock garden or borders.
Prop: D or S

G. himalayense ★ (syns. *G. grandiflorum* and *G. meeboldii*)
Himalayas. 12-18in (30-45cm). June.
Excellent weed smothering, spreading ground cover. Handsome finely cut leaves taking on brilliant autumn tints. Flowers 2in (5cm), saucer-shaped, violet blue flushed reddish pink, produced spasmodically after main flowering until autumn. Needs space to spread under trees or shrubs. Lovely with yellows, pinks and purples.
Prop: D

G. h. 'Gravetye' Somewhat shorter with smaller leaves and larger flowers, the reddish central zone being more pronounced.

G. h. 'Irish Blue' Introduced by Mr Graham Thomas from Eire, flowers are a beautiful pale blue, with even larger central zone. Hardly ever without flowers from June to October.

G. h. 'Plenum' (syn. *G. h.* 'Birch Double') Small rounded leaves; flowers 1in (2.5cm) soft lilac blue, fully double, flushed with pink. A charming little plant (10in/25cm), not very vigorous, sun or part shade, where not too dry.
Prop: D (sterile)

G. ibericum subsp. *ibericum* NE Turkey, Caucasus. 18in (45cm). June.
Handsomely divided leaves with divisions overlapping; numerous lobes
and teeth. Flowers 1½-2in (approx. 5cm) deep violet with darker, feathered
veins and notched petals. Flowering period rather short, but often produces a few blooms in autumn. Border or under shrubs in sun.
Prop: D or S

G. **'Johnson's Blue'** * *(G. himalayense × G. pratense)*
12-18in (30-45cm). June onwards.
Leafy, spreading clumps of elegant, finely cut foliage, providing dense
ground cover - a strong grower. Flowers 2in (5cm), good lavender blue,
tinged pink at centre, fluttering well above the foliage.
Prop: D (sterile)

G. **'Kate'** (syn. *G.* 'Kate Folkard'), (*G. endressii × G. sessiliflorum*)
4-6in (10-15cm). June onwards
This hybrid appeared in the garden of Revd Oliver Folkard in Lincolnshire and is named after his daughter. A delightful dwarf plant with small,
rounded, cut leaves of bronzy green similar to those of *G. sessiliflorum*
'Nigricans'. Sepals also tinged with brown. Flowers ½-¾in (approx.
1.5cm), funnel-shaped, pale pink with dark veins on thin trailing stems.
Rock garden, scree, trough or alpine house. Tends to die out and may need
winter protection.
Prop: D (sterile)

G. kishtvariense Kashmir. 12in (30cm). All summer.
A recent introduction by Roy Lancaster (1978). A bushy plant, creeping
by underground stolons. Leaves deeply divided with few broad lobes,
bright green and wrinkled. Flowers 1½in (approx. 4cm), facing upwards
on thin stems, rich purple, white at centre and finely veined. Prefers some
shade. Woodland or shady corner.
Prop: D or S

G. krameri N. China, CIS, Korea, Japan. July-September.
Distinctive leaves, very deeply cut with narrow coarsely serrated lobes.
Flowers 1-1¼in (approx. 3cm). flat, rose pink with darker veins on long
trailing thin, rather lax, stems. Prefers shade in woodland or wild garden.
Interesting but no real garden value.
Prop: S

G. lambertii (syn. *G. grevilleanum*) Himalayas. 12-18in (30-45cm).
Late summer
Trailing plant with few basal leaves. Leaves wrinkled with sharply pointed
lobes. Flowers 1-1¼ (approx. 3cm), nodding, saucer-shaped, very delicate
pale pink with crimson veining converging into central crimson stain.

Strikingly beautiful, though sometimes reluctant to flower. Best scrambling through other plants or shrubs in partial shade.
Prop: S

G. l. 'Swansdown' The exquisite white flowered form: the flowers flushed pink with crimson centres and very pale veins. Leaves mottled with two shades of green.
Prop: S (which comes true)

G. libani (syn. *G. libanoticum*) Lebanon, W. Syria, C. & S. Turkey. 15in (40cm). April-May.
An unusual geranium, leaves shiny dark green with pale veins; rather widely spaced divisions. Flowers 1½in (approx. 4cm) violet blue, notched petals and feathery veins. Dormant after flowering, until autumn. The thick roots tend to lie on the surface of the soil and benefit from a mulch, especially in drought conditions. A charmer for the large rock garden, or near front of the border where later flowering plants can fill the gap.
Prop: D or S

G. × lindavicum (*G. argenteum × G. cinereum*)

G. × l. 'Apple Blossom' (syn. *G. × l.* 'Jenny Bloom')
From Blooms of Bressingham. Neat clumps 6in (15cm) of small, deeply cut, silvery leaves. Flowers (June-August) palest pink, lightly veined — delightful! Rock garden, scree, trough or alpine house in well-drained gritty soil. Protect from winter wet.

G. × l. 'Alanah' Described by the late Walter Ingwersen (1946) as "a very attractive plant, but slightly less silvery in foliage than *G. argenteum* and extremely free in the production of its vivid crimson-purple flowers. It is shy to increase". He considered it to be the same plant as *G. argenteum purpureum*.

G. × l. 'Lissadell' (syn. *G. × l.* 'Lissadell Purple') Compact hummocks of small silvery-green foliage topped by deep plum-coloured flowers — most attractive. Lived for twelve years in a trough in Surrey.
Prop: C or RC (not easy)

G. macrorrhizum ★ S. Europe. 12-18in (30-45cm). May-June.
Reliable ground cover, spreading by underground rhizomes. Copious foliage, almost evergreen. Leaves divided, rounded, sticky and aromatic. Good autumn colour. Flowers 1in (2.5cm), dull magenta, reddish bladder-like calyx. A strong grower, but not too rampant. Sun or shade.
Prop: D

G. m. album Lovely white-flowered form with faint pink flush.

G. m. 'Bevan's Variety' Good deep magenta flowers, rather spoilt by red sepals.

G. m. 'Czakor' Flowers deep magenta pink, an improvement on 'Bevan's Variety'.

G. m. 'Ingwersen's Variety' One of the prettiest forms with soft pink flowers and paler leaves.

G. m. 'Variegatum' Greyish-green leaves splashed with cream. Purplish-pink flowers. Not so vigorous as any of the above, needing regular feeding and some sun. Hopefully someone will raise a white flowered form.

G. macrostylum Greece, Albania, S. of the former Yugoslavia, C. & W. Turkey. 9in (22cm). May-June.
A pretty plant, spreading rapidly by small tubers. Leaves small and finely cut, dying down after flowering until autumn. Flowers 1in (2.5cm), rather frail, mauvish pink with darker veins and centre. There are also lavender-blue forms, net veined but not dark at the centre. Can be a nuisance in the rock garden; best confined to paving or grown in containers.
Prop: T

G. maculatum NE America. 24-30in (60-75cm). May-July.
Erect plant from strong rootstock. Handsomely fingered, shiny leaves. Flowers 1in (2.5cm), shallow bowl-shaped in clusters, usually pale lilac pink, but can be deeper. Petals notched, white at base. Prefers moist soil in border, stream-side or wild garden in sun or part shade.
Prop: D or S

G. m. album A desirable white form, more difficult to cultivate.

G. maderense Madeira. 36-48in (19-120cm). February-March onwards.
A magnificent, architectural giant, growing from an impressive rosette of very large, much divided leaves on brownish-red stems. Flowers 1½in (approx. 4cm), massed well above the foliage, purplish pink with pale netted veins, dark crimson centre and dark red anthers. Makes a wonderful pot plant, needing winter protection in a greenhouse. May behave as a biennial, dying after flowering, but sometimes grows on from side shoots. Initial growth is rapid and young plants need frequent potting-on, so as not to check their progress.
Prop: S (after storing for a month or two)

G. x magnificum ★ (*G. ibericum* x *G. platypetalum*) 24in (60cm). June.
A vigorous hybrid, superior to both parents. Leaves nearer to *G. platypetalum*, colouring well in autumn. Flowers 2in (5cm), saucer-shaped, rich violet, darkly veined and produced in abundance, magnificent in its few weeks of glory. Excellent ground cover under shrubs in sun or half shade.

Lovely with *Iris pallida*, blue grasses and yellow roses.
Prop: D (sterile)

G. malviflorum *G. atlanticum* misapplied. S. Spain, Morocco,
Algeria. 9-12in (22-30cm). March-April.
A tuberous rooted geranium. Leaves prettily rounded and finely cut.
Flowers 1½in (4cm), violet blue with reddish veins, giving a shot-silk
appearance. Poor soil in sun.
Prop: T

G. 'Mavis Simpson' see *G. riversleaianum*

G. × **monacense** (syn. *G. punctatum* of gardens), (*G. phaeum* × *G. reflexum*)
Good ground cover with characteristics midway between both parents.
Leaves usually blotched with brown. Flowers with strongly reflexed
petals, dull mauvish purple with central white and violet zone.

Geranium × *monacense*

G. × *monacense nothovar anglicum* (*G. phaeum lividum* × *G. reflexum*)
Flowers pale lilac pink, small white central area with wider violet zone, strongly veined.

G. × *monacense* '**Muldoon**' A clone with very striking, strongly dark-blotched leaves.

G. *nepalense* E. Afghanistan, Himalayas, China.
A weedy species related to *G. thunbergii*; of no real garden value except perhaps in the wild garden. Dark evergreen leaves usually blotched with purplish brown. Flowers ½in (approx. 1cm), white to pale pink on thin trailing stems. Self-sown seedlings can be a nuisance.

G. *nervosum* (syns. *G. strigosum* and *G. viscosissimum* var. *nervosum*).
NW America. 12-18in (30-45cm). May onwards.
A variable plant bearing a strong resemblance to *G. viscosissimum* with the same sticky hairy characteristics, though the basal leaves are smaller. These are light green and broadly fingered with few, smaller stem leaves. Flowers, borne on a single stem, are branched at the top, 1-1¾in (2-4cm), flat, pale pink to reddish purple with notched petals and dark veins. Some years ago Blooms of Bressingham were offering a small form under the name *G. incisum* (which belongs strictly to *G. oreganum*). Its flowers were a lovely deep rose pink with finely pencilled crimson veins, but numerous self-sown seedlings were generally of poor colour. Border or wild garden in sun or shade. Will grow in dry shade under trees or shrubs.
Prop: D or S

G. *nodosum* * Central France to Pyrenees, C. Italy, C. of the former Yugoslavia. 12in (30cm). Spring to autumn.
A modestly charming geranium for woodland or shady border; will colonize under trees in dry soil. Flowers funnel-shaped ¾-1in (approx. 2cm), lilac pink with notched petals. Hardly out of flower all summer. There is also a pink flowered form.
Prop: D or S (self-sows in moderation)

G. *oreganum* W. USA. 24in (60cm). June-July.
A lovely plant with leaves similar to *G. pratense* making substantial clumps. Flowers 1¾-2in (approx. 5cm), saucer-shaped and upwardly inclined, deep rose purple and prolific. Border in sun or part shade.
Prop: D or S

G. *orientalitibeticum* G. *stapfianum roseum* misapplied. SW China.
8in (20cm). June-July.
Tuberous rooted. Pretty marbled leaves. Flowers 1in (2.5cm), purplish pink with white centre. Somewhat invasive and best contained in pockets between paving stones.
Prop: T

26

G. × *oxonianum* ★ (*G. endressii* × *G. versicolor*)

G. × *o.* **'A. T. Johnson'** Slightly shorter than *G. endressii* at 12in (30cm). Flowers delicate silvery pink, very freely produced.

G. × *o.* **'Claridge Druce'** 18-24in (45-60cm). Extremely vigorous; handsome greyish-green foliage. Flowers large, trumpet-shaped, deep rose pink, strongly veined. An ideal weed smothering ground cover, but should only be introduced to the small garden with caution. Grows practically anywhere!
Prop: D or S (seedlings may vary, but self-sows with abandon)

G. × *o.* **'Rose Clair'** 18-24in (45-60cm). Described by Walter Ingwersen as "a clear rose-salmon with just a trace of veining and similar habit to *G.* 'A. T. Johnson'." Unfortunately plants with white veiny flowers are often sold under this name.

G. × *o.* **'Southcombe Double'** 15in (40cm). Originated at Southcombe Garden Plant Nursery in Devon. Flowers ¾in (2cm), semi-double, warm pink similar to *G.* 'Wargrave Pink' — a pretty plant. Not so vigorous as other oxonianum hybrids.
Prop: D (sterile)

G. × *o.* **'Southcombe Star'** Previously thought to be the same as *G.* × *o.* 'Southcombe Double' but has a more sprawling habit and bluish-pink starry flowers.
Prop: D (sterile)

G. × *o.* **'Thurstonianum'** 18-24in (45-60cm). Flowers with very narrow curiously twisted petals, reddish purple, white at the base and deeply notched. Foliage sometimes blotched, but plants are variable. Interesting rather than beautiful.

G. × *o.* **'Winscombe'** 18in (45cm). Discovered by the late Margery Fish in a Somerset garden; similar in habit to *G. endressii*. Flowers open very pale silvery pink, darkening with age to deep pink, creating a delightful two-tone effect.

G. *palmatum* (syn. *G. anemonifolium*) Madeira. 14-36in (35-90cm). Summer.
Resembles *G.canariense*, but with hardly any rosette stem and greener stalks. Rosettes very large, leaves can be 12in (30cm) or more across. Flowers 1-1½in (approx. 3cm), very prolific, mauvish pink, crimson centre. Needs winter protection in all but the warmest areas. Makes a showy pot-plant.
Prop: S

G. *palustre* ★ E. and C. Europe. 12-18in (30-45cm). All summer.
A low growing, bushy plant. Basal leaves light green, remaining fresh look-

ing even in drought conditions. Flowers 1-1½in (approx. 3cm), trumpet-shaped bright magenta pink, with dark veins, white at the centre and violet anthers. Useful in the border for its long flowering period, trailing over plants that are out of flower.
Prop: S (self-sows freely)

G. peloponnesiacum Greece. 18-24in (45-60cm). May-June.
Pretty, velvety wrinkled leaves dying down after flowering, re-appearing in autumn. Flowers 1½in (4cm), clusters on long stems, upward facing, slatey blue. Petals deeply notched and veiny. A dainty plant for rock garden or border.
Prop: S

G. phaeum * Mountains of S. & C. Europe. 24in (60cm). May-July.
The mourning widow geranium, so called because of its unusually dark, nodding flowers. Leaves divided and sometimes blotched with purplish brown in the notches. Flowers 1in (2.5cm), flattish, very sombre dark maroon, white at centre. Petals often slightly frilled round the edge. Excellent for quite dry shady areas, where it will colonize and hybridize where other forms are grown.

G. p. 'Album' A delightful pure white.

G. p. 'Lily Lovell' A beautiful large flowered form of rich purple mauve, raised by Trevor Bath in Woking, Surrey.

G. p. var. lividum Very pale lilac.

G. p. 'Variegatum' Leaves splashed irregularly with cream and touches of bright, reddish pink. All are quaint and graceful.
Prop: D or S (variable)

G. platyanthum (syn. *G. eriostemon*) NE Asia, E. Tibet, W. China, Korea and Japan. 18-24in (45-60cm). May-June.
A handsome, hairy geranium with large, wrinkled shallowly lobed leaves, colouring well in the autumn. Flowers 1-1½in (approx. 3cm), nearly flat, in dense clusters on erect stems; slatey mauvish pink with small white centre. Sometimes disparagingly described as 'muddy coloured' or 'ill defined purple' though it can be both interesting and pleasing. Border, woodland, wild garden in sun or part shade.
Prop: D or S

G. platypetalum Caucasus. 12-18in (30-45cm). June-July.
A hairy plant somewhat similar to *G. ibericum*, but leaves not so deeply cut and less sharply toothed. Flowers 1½in (4cm), deep violet blue with strong dark veins. Border and ground cover in sun or part shade.
Prop: D or S

G. pogonanthum SW China, W. & N. Burma. 18-24in (45-60cm). July-September.
Very attractive both in leaf and flower. Forms clumps of lightish-green, marbled leaves. Flowers 1-1½in (approx. 3cm), dusky pink with narrow, reflexed petals like small cyclamen. Beautiful and unusual. Takes a year or two to establish and then needs regular replanting if the roots work their way to the surface. Border, wild garden. Sun or shade.
Prop: D or S

G. polyanthes Himalayas, SW China. 15-18in (38-45cm). July.
Grows from knobbly brown tuber-like roots, which tend to push their way out of the soil and need recovering. Leaves small, rounded, divided and fleshy. Flowers 1in (2.5cm) funnel-shaped, very bright shiny pink. A pretty plant for large rock garden, but difficult to keep in cultivation, often dying out after two or three years.
Prop: S (easy)

G. pratense * N. Europe, Asia. 24-36in (60-90cm). June-July.
Our well-loved meadow cranesbill, a wonderful sight when colonizing vast areas of roadside. It will do the same in the garden, making large clumps of handsomely divided leaves and quantities of saucer-shaped flowers 1½in (4cm) in lovely shades from deep violet blue, pink, pale blue and white with varying degrees of veining, borne on tall branching stems. Border (may need support), meadow, light woodland. There are a number of desirable garden forms.
Prop: D (seed will be variable, though all but the doubles are prolific seeders)

G. p. forma albiflorum The name for the white flowered forms, both wild and cultivated.

G. p. 'Galactic' Rather shorter, darker leaf and pure, milky white flowers.

G. p. 'Mrs Kendall Clark' An exquisite shade of pearly blue grey, flushed with soft pink.

G. p. 'Plenum Album' Rather small, loosely petalled rosettes of 'off white' flowers tinged with violet. Not easy to grow, needing rich soil and regular dividing.
Prop: D (sterile)

G. p. 'Plenum Caeruleum' Copious loosely petalled rosettes of lavender-blue flowers tinged with pink, over a long period from June to August. Prone to mildew in dry soil. Benefits from regular division. Lovely with grey or silver leaved plants — a 'must' for the border!
Prop: D (sterile)

G. p. 'Plenum Violaceum' (probably syn. *G. p.* 'Purpureum Plenum') Perfectly formed tight pompoms of rich violet, a bit later than *G. p.* 'Plenum Caeruleum', not quite so vigorous.
Prop: D (sterile)

G. p. 'Silver Queen' A tall, strong growing plant of palest silvery blue, but the description from the Wisley Trials Report, "white with a tinge of very pale violet" seems to be nearer the plant generally sold under this name. Some forms are enhanced by prominent black anthers.

G. p. 'Striatum' (syn. *G. p.* 'Bicolor') Interesting and attractive variant. Flowers basically white, erraticaly streaked with violet.
Prop: S (comes true)

G. procurrens ★   Himalayas. July onwards.
Low growing, rampant ground cover for dry areas. Sending out very long prostrate stems, which root at the leaf joints. Leaves wrinked and faintly marbled. Flowers 1in (2.5cm) dull purple, black at centre. Will weave through shrubs or cover large areas under specimen trees. This geranium should carry a warning 'Beware of Take Over'!
Prop: rooted pieces easily transplanted

G. psilostemon ★ (syn. *G. armenum*) NE Turkey, SW Caucasus. 36-48in (90-120cm).   June-August.
A stunning border plant with elegant, very large, deeply cut leaves, turning brilliant red in autumn. Flowers 1½in (approx. 4cm), bowl-shaped, intense magenta crimson accentuated by a black central zone and dark veins. Best in sun but will tolerate some shade. Can be toned down by planting in association with pastel shades and silver foliage. *G. p.* 'Bressingham Flair' is a paler form, lilac pink and a little shorter.
Prop: D or S

G. pylzowianum W. China.   6-10in (15-25cm).   May-June.
Travels rapidly by chains of small tubers. Leaves rounded, finely dissected. Flowers 1in (approx. 2cm), deep clear pink. Can be a pest in the rock garden, and best kept away from precious plants: in containers, paving or edge of path in sun.
Prop: T

G. pyrenaicum SW & W. Europe. 12in (30cm). May onwards.
Mounds of nicely rounded, evergreen leaves. Flowers ¾in (2cm), mauvish pink with notched petals freely produced on thin stems. Rather too weedy for anything but the wild garden. *G. p.* forma *albiflorum* is a pretty, starry white flowered form.
Prop: S (self sows abundantly)

G. reflexum Italy, the former Yugoslavia, N. Greece. 18-24in (45-60cm). May-June.
Similar to *G. phaeum* with fresh green leaves, usually blotched dark purplish brown where divisions meet. Flowers ¾in (2cm), nodding rosey mauve, strongly reflexed, narrow petals, white at base. Ground cover or shady corner.
Prop: D or S

G. refractum Himalayas, N. Burma, SW China. 18-24in (45-60cm).
Not in cultivation until recently, but seed from Nepal now being distributed. Deeply divided, sometimes marbled leaves. Flowers nodding, white or pink, narrow reflexed petals, red stamens. Distinguished by purple glandular hairs on the upper parts.

G. renardii Caucasus. 12in (30cm). June.
A lovely foliage plant. Leaves a soft sage green, velvety to the touch, with a distinctive scalloped shape. Flowers large, white, etched with purple veins. Petals widely spaced. Often a shy flowerer, said to do better in poor soil in sun or part shade. Rock garden, low wall, paving, front of the border.

G. r. 'Whiteknights' A lilac-blue form.
Prop: D or S

G. richardsonii Western N. America. 12-24in (30-60cm). May onwards.
Pleasing clumps of deeply divided, shiny green leaves with pointed lobes. Flowers 1-1½in (approx. 3cm), flat white or tinged with pink, lightly veined. Likes plenty of moisture in wild garden or pondside in sun.
Prop: D or S

G. × *riversleaianum* (*G. endressii* × *G.traversii*)

G. × r. 'Mavis Simpson' Makes wide mats of 9in (22cm) high grey-green leaves covered with endless, silvery shell-pink flowers on thin trailing stems all summer into autumn. Seems to be hardier than *G. × r.* 'Russell Prichard'. Front of the border, rock garden, low wall or bank in sun. Lovely with purple foliage plants.
Prop: D (sterile)

G. × r. 'Russell Prichard' 8in (20cm) mounds of small silvery grey-green foliage. Flowers 1¼in (3cm), bright magenta pink on trailing stems, prolifically produced from July onwards. Not reliably hardy. Try planting at a slight downward angle beneath overhanging rock to protect crowns from winter wet. Similar situations to *G.* 'Mavis Simpson'.
Prop: D (sterile)

G. *rubescens* (biennial) Madeira. 24-36in (60-90cm).
May onwards.
Resembles a large herb robert. Flower and leaf stalks beetroot red from impressive rosette. Flowers 1in (2.5cm) numerous, bright pink with dark centre. Reasonably hardy in a sheltered corner in light soil, sun or shade, naturalising where happy. Sometimes affected by virus which distorts the petals (in which case the plants should be destroyed).

G. 'Russell Prichard' see *G.* × *riversleaianum*

G. *sanguineum* ★ Europe, Caucasus, N. Turkey. 9-12in (22-30cm).
May onwards.
The bloody cranesbill, though not blood-red! Forms wide mats of tangled, leafy stems. Leaves small, rounded, finely cut, turning brilliant shades in autumn. Flowers 1-1½in (approx. 3cm), saucer-shaped, purple magenta all summer. Front of the border, rock garden, low walls, paving.
Prop: D or S (seedlings variable)

Geranium sanguineum

32

G. s. 'Album' A good pure white, taller than the type, rather spindly stems and less compact.

G. s. 'Glenluce' Discovered by A. T. Johnson in Scotland. Beautiful, large rose-pink flowers.

G. s. 'Holden' (syn. *G. s.* 'Holden's Variety') Close mats of small leaves and bright pure pink flowers.

G. s. 'Jubilee Pink' Raised by Jack Drake in Scotland. Compact growth, bright magenta pink flowers.

G. s. var. *striatum* (syn. *G. lancastriense*) One of the best from Walney Island in Lancashire (now Cumbria). Large, very pale pink flowers (almost white) with pink veins, non-stop all summer until the frosts.

G. sessiliflorum subsp. *novae-zelandiae* New Zealand.
3in (aprox. 7cm). June onwards.
Neat rosettes of small rounded green leaves and tiny ½in (1cm) white flowers. Rock garden, scree, trough or gravel path.
Prop: S

G. s. 'Nigricans' * A fascinating dark-leaved form, varying from pale bronze to very dark brown. Self-sows moderately. Seems to like the peat bed.

G. shikokianum S. Japan, Korea. 8-16in (20-40cm). July onwards.
Compact clumps of deeply cut, light green leaves, often with yellowish-green marbling, pale and glossy on the under sides. Good autumn colour. Flowers on longish stems, funnel-shaped, 1in (2.5cm) pink with white central area, netted with purple veins. Dislikes hot, dry conditions, best in shade, scrambling through low shrubs.
Prop: D or S

G. sibiricum E. & C. Europe, CIS, China, Japan, W. Himalayas.
A weedy sprawling plant with light green leaves and small ½in (1cm) white or pale pink flowers. No real garden value.

G. sinense SW China. 24in (60cm). July-August.
A fascinating and unusual plant of great distinction. Leaves deeply divided, shiny olive green and faintly marbled, on reddish stems. Flowers ¾in (2cm) similar in shape to *G. phaeum* very dark (almost black) velvety reflexed petals, coral at the base, black anthers and crimson-red stigma; deserves close inspection. Plants rather slow to establish, building up to a substantial mound. Shade and moist soil.
Prop: D or S

G. soboliferum CIS, Manchuria, mountains of C. & S. Japan.
12-15in (30-40cm). July-Sept.
Small clumps of finely cut feathery leaves. Flowers 1½in (4cm), saucer-

shaped, reddish purple with dark veins, notched petals. Needs plenty of moisture in full sun.
Prop: D or S.

G. stapfianum   SW China, SE Tibet.   6in (15cm).   June.
A dwarf plant, spreading by underground stolons. Leaves small, kidney-shaped, deeply cut and marbled. Leaf and flower stalks red. Flowers 1½in (4cm), saucer-shaped, deep magenta with dark red veins and notched petals. Not an easy plant in cultivation. Rock garden, scree, alpine house. (This is not the geranium sold as *G. stapfianum roseum* for which see *G. orientalitibeticum.*)
Prop: D or S

G. swatense   Swat division of Pakistan.   12in (30cm).   All summer.
A low growing, sprawling plant from a thick tap root, mottled leaves on long thin reddish stems. Flowers 1½in (4cm) rather flat, purplish pink with purple anthers, but variable. Not easy to please and liable to die out. Rock garden or wall in sun or part shade.
Prop: D or S

G. sylvaticum *   Europe, N. Turkey.   24-30in (60-75cm).
May-June and often later.
The wood cranesbill. An upright geranium developing fine clumps of broadly fingered, lightish green leaves, attractively lobed and toothed. Flowers 1in (2.5cm) saucer-shaped, purplish violet with white centres, in profusion.

G. s. 'Album'   18in (45cm), a beautiful pure white form with large pale green leaves. A valuable addition to the White Garden.

G. s. 'Mayflower' An improved clone with larger, pale violet blue, white-centred flowers. Lovely with spring flowers and bulbs.

G. s. forma roseum a natural pink variant. An especially good form introduced from the Swiss Alps by Mr W. A. Baker with larger, shell-pink blooms and a long flowering period — generally known as *G. s.* 'Baker's Pink'.

G. s.'Wanneri' has flowers of plummy pink with rose red veins.
Prop: D or S (seedlings will be variable though *G.s.*'Album' seems to come true)

G. thunbergii   N. China, Taiwan, Japan.   9in (22cm).   July-October.
A vigorous, sprawling plant. Leaves lightish green with dark blotches, where divisions meet. Semi-evergreen. Flowers ½-¾in (approx. 1.5cm) varying from white to purplish pink over a long period. Rather weedy but useful ground cover for dry shade.
Prop: D or S

G. traversii var. elegans   Chatham Islands.   6-8in (15-20cm).
June-September.
Compact rosettes of silver green, beautifully fashioned cut leaves. Flowers
1in (2.5cm), saucer-shaped, lovely milky pink and finely veined on leafy
stems which tend to flop and lie on the surface of the soil. Rock garden,
scree, alpine house in well-drained gritty soil in full sun. Not completely
hardy, needing some protection in winter.
Prop: S (self-sown seedlings occasionally appear)

G. tuberosum   Mediterranean.   8-10in (20-25cm).   May.
Grows from moderately spreading tubers, sending up finely cut ferny
leaves in spring, dying down in summer. Flowers 1in (2.5cm), purplish
pink with darker veins on erect stems. Rock garden or scree in sun.
Prop: D or S

G. versicolor ★ (syn. *G. striatum*) Europe. 18in (45cm). May.
A bushy plant similar to *G. endressii* forming hummocks of light green,
blotched leaves which remain fresh in winter. Dainty flowers, trumpet-
shaped 1in (2.5cm), white with a network of fine magenta veins. Good
ground cover for sun or shade. Hybridizes freely with *G. endressii*.
Prop: D (seedlings will be variable)

G. viscosissimum   Western N. America.   12-24in (30-60cm).
June and often later.
An attractive, sticky plant with large hairy divided leaves and sharply
toothed segments, similar to *G. nervosum*. Flowers 1¼-1½in (approx. 3cm),
bright rose pink to purple in clusters on strong branching stems. Border
in sun.
Prop: D or S.

G. wallichianum 'Buxton's Variety' (syn. *G. w.* 'Buxton's Blue')
Himalayas.   12in (30cm).   July onwards.
Originated in the garden of E. C. Buxton in N. Wales. A great favourite,
having long, leafy trailing stems. Leaves shallowly divided and marbled.
Flowers 1-1½ (approx. 3cm) saucer-shaped, beautiful sky blue with large,
clean white centre. Although said to require a cool root run, it has thrived
and flowered prolifically in hot, dry summers. Rock garden, under shrubs,
trailing over low walls.
Prop: S (comes true, but advisable to select seedlings with best blue
flowers)

G. wlassovianum ★   E. Siberia, Mongolia, Far East, CIS,
N. China.   12-18in   (30-45cm).   July-August.
A clump former with attractive foliage emerging pinkish bronze in spring.
Mature leaves dusky green tinged with brown, velvety in texture, assuming
brilliant red autumn colour, darkening to purplish brown before dying

away. Flowers 1¼-1½in (approx. 3cm), deep purple violet with darker feathered veins and small white central area. Border, wild garden, ground cover where not excessively dry.
Prop: D or S

G. yesoense   C. & N. Japan, Kuril Islands.   12-18in (30-45cm). June-August.
A bushy plant similar to *G. dahuricum*. Leaves very deeply and sharply cut. Flowers 1¼in (approx. 3cm), saucer-shaped, pink with darker veins, or white. Not a particularly garden worthy plant, but suitable for light woodland or wild garden in moisture retentive soil.
Prop: D or S

G. yunnanense   SW China, N. Burma. 18-24in (45-60cm). June-July.
Compact rootstock, leaves deeply divided, yellowish green and marbled. Flowers 1-1½in (approx. 3cm), nodding, bowl-shaped, a lovely deep pink with dark anthers, not easy to grow in south of England. Flowering stems lax. Woodland or wild garden. Sun or part shade.
Prop: D or S

SOUTH AFRICAN SPECIES

In recent years several perennial species from South Africa have been tried in the British Isles and a few have proved to be hardier than one would imagine.

G. caffrum 24in (60cm). Summer.
Grows from thick taproot; stems slender, woody at the base. Leaves very deeply cut with narrow lobes and sharply toothed. Flowers small but prolific, usually white, sometimes pink with shallowly notched petals. Reasonably hardy in light soil.
Prop: C or S (self sows quite freely)

G. incanum var. **multifidum**   8in (20cm).   All summer.
Forms low tussocks of very finely cut feathery leaves, dark green above, silvery beneath. Flowers 1in (2.5cm), deep reddish purple with darker veins, white at centre. Good trailing over edge of troughs or sprawling over rocks in sun. Not reliably hardy.
Prop: C (need protection in winter) S (self-sown seedlings sometimes appear)

G. pulchrum   36in (90cm).   July-August.
A lovely foliage sub-shrub. Stems woody and quite thick at the base. Leaves soft, velvety, silvery grey green, undersides covered with silvery silky hairs — almost white; handsomely fingered and sharply serrated. Flowers 1-1½in (approx. 3cm), mauvish-pink, sometimes white at centre. Has survived four winters outside in Somerset and -6° C or more of frost!

Sun or light shade. Border or bank.
Prop: C or S

G. robustum   24in (60cm).   All summer.
A reasonably hardy sub-shrub, stems woody at the base. Lovely ferny grey-green leaves silvery on the underside. Flowers 1-1½in (approx. 3cm), mauvish pink or pale purple, shallowly notched petals. Withstands drought well and has survived outside for the past six years in Somerset, before that several years in Surrey. Border in sun. Effective with red-leaved berberis, *Heuchera* 'Palace Purple' and *Crocus speciosus*.
Prop: C or S (self sows occasionally)

ANNUALS

There are a number of annual geraniums, several of which are really only of interest to the collector, having very small flowers and weedy habits. Space within this booklet is limited, so descriptions are confined to two personal favourites. However, I must mention the herb robert, *G. robertianum* so pretty and delightful in both pink and white forms. I would not like to be without it, but there are times when I curse its proliferation! *G. r.* 'Celtic White' is smaller, forming rosettes of pale green, parsley-like leaves. It has small, pure white flowers, but is equally generous with its seedlings.

Geranium robertianum

G. *brutium* Italy, Sicily, Balkan Peninsular, Turkey. 12in (30cm).
April-August.
One of the best annual species, bright and cheerful, developing pleasant
mounds of small light-green, rounded leaves. Flowers ¾-1in (approx.
2cm), bright rose pink in profusion on thin trailing stems for many weeks.
Often starts flowering in March. Best in sun. Border or wild garden.
Prop: S (self-sows in moderation)

G. *lucidum* Europe, Africa, SW & C. China. 12in (30cm).
Spring-summer.
The shining cranesbill. Delightful, but very free with offspring. As these
are usually confined around the parent plant it makes pretty ground cover
for inhospitable dry areas under trees or shrubs. Rosettes of small rounded,
succulent leaves on red stems, building up to 12in (30cm), but usually less
in poor soil. Flowers ½in (approx. 1cm) deep pink. Some rosettes will be
present in winter if germination has taken place in autumn.

REFERENCES

W. Ingwersen *The Genus Geranium* 1946.
Dr Peter F. Yeo *Hardy Geraniums* 1992.

Nurseries Specializing in Hardy Geraniums

Axletree Nursery (David and Frances Hibberd)
Starvecrow Lane, Peasmarsh, Rye, E.Sussex TN31 6XL.

Birkheads Cottage Garden Nursery (Mrs Christine Liddle)
Birkheads Lane, Nr Sunniside, Newcastle upon Tyne, Tyne and Wear NE16 5EL

Bressingham Gardens (Blooms) Diss, Norfolk IP22 2AB. MO*

Catforth Gardens (Judith Bradshaw & Chris Moore)
Roots Lane, Catforth, Preston, Lancs. PR4 OJB

Charter House Nursery (John Ross)
2 Nunwood, Stepford Road, Dumfries and Galloway, Scotland DG2 7RE. MO

Coombland Gardens (Mrs Rosemary Lee)
Coombland, Coneyhurst, Billingshust, W.Sussex. MO

Cranesbill Nursery (Mrs S.M.Bates)
White Cottage, Stock Green, Nr Redditch, Worcestershire. MO

Elworthy Cottage Plants (Mrs J.Spiller)
Elworthy Cottage, Lydeard St Lawrence, Taunton, Somerset TA4 3PX

Donington Plants (D.W.Salt)
Donington House, Main Road, Wrangle, Boston, Lincolnshire PE22 9AT. MO

Glebe Cottage Plants (Carol Klein)
Pixie Lane, Warkleigh, Umberleigh, N.Devon EX37 9DH. MO

Henllys Lodge Plants (Mrs E.Lane)
Henllys Lodge, Beaumaris, Anglesey, Gwynedd, LL58 8RU. MO

Holden Clough Nursery (P.J.Foley)
Holden, Bolton-by-Bowland, Clithroe, Lancashire BB7 4PF. MO

The Margery Fish Plant Nursery (M.Stainer)
East Lambrook Manor, East Lambrook, S Petherton, Somerset TA13 5HL. MO

The Nursery Further Afield (Gerald and Mary Sinclair)
Mixbury, Brackley, Northants NN13 5YR.

Spinners (Peter Chappell) Boldre, Lymington, Hants SO41 5QE

Stillingfleet Lodge Nurseries (Vanessa Cook)
Stillingfleet, Yorkshire, YO4 6HW. MO

Unusual Plants (Beth Chatto)
Beth Chatto Gardens, Elmstead Market. Colchester, Essex CO7 7DB. MO

Washfield Nursery (Elizabeth Strangman)
Horn's Road, Hawkhurst, Kent TN18 4QV.

* MO = Mail order available

Glossary

C	Cuttings.
CIS	Formerly the USSR.
D	Division.
forma	form.
misapplied	incorrect name used by gardeners.
MO	Mail order.
Prop.	Propagation.
RC	Root cuttings.
S	Seed.
subsp.	subspecies.
syn.	synonymous, a former name for the species.
T	Tubers.
var.	naturally occurring.
★	Easy geraniums for beginners

Notes

Notes